For Victor, my hope-warrior.
And for those who silently
work to heal the broken places.
I see you.

- Jo

For Zach
- LZ

I Can Be an Instrument of Peace
Text copyright © 2021 Mary Jo Burchard
Illustrations copyright © 2021 Leanna Zeibak
All rights reserved.
No part of this book may be used or reproduced in any manner whatsoever
without written permission except in the case of brief quotes in critical articles and reviews.
For information address Neoteny Books.
www.neotenybooks.com

ISBN: 978-0-578-99884-8

First Edition

I Can Be an Instrument of Peace

Mary Jo Burchard and Leanna Zeibak

Somebody needs to do something.

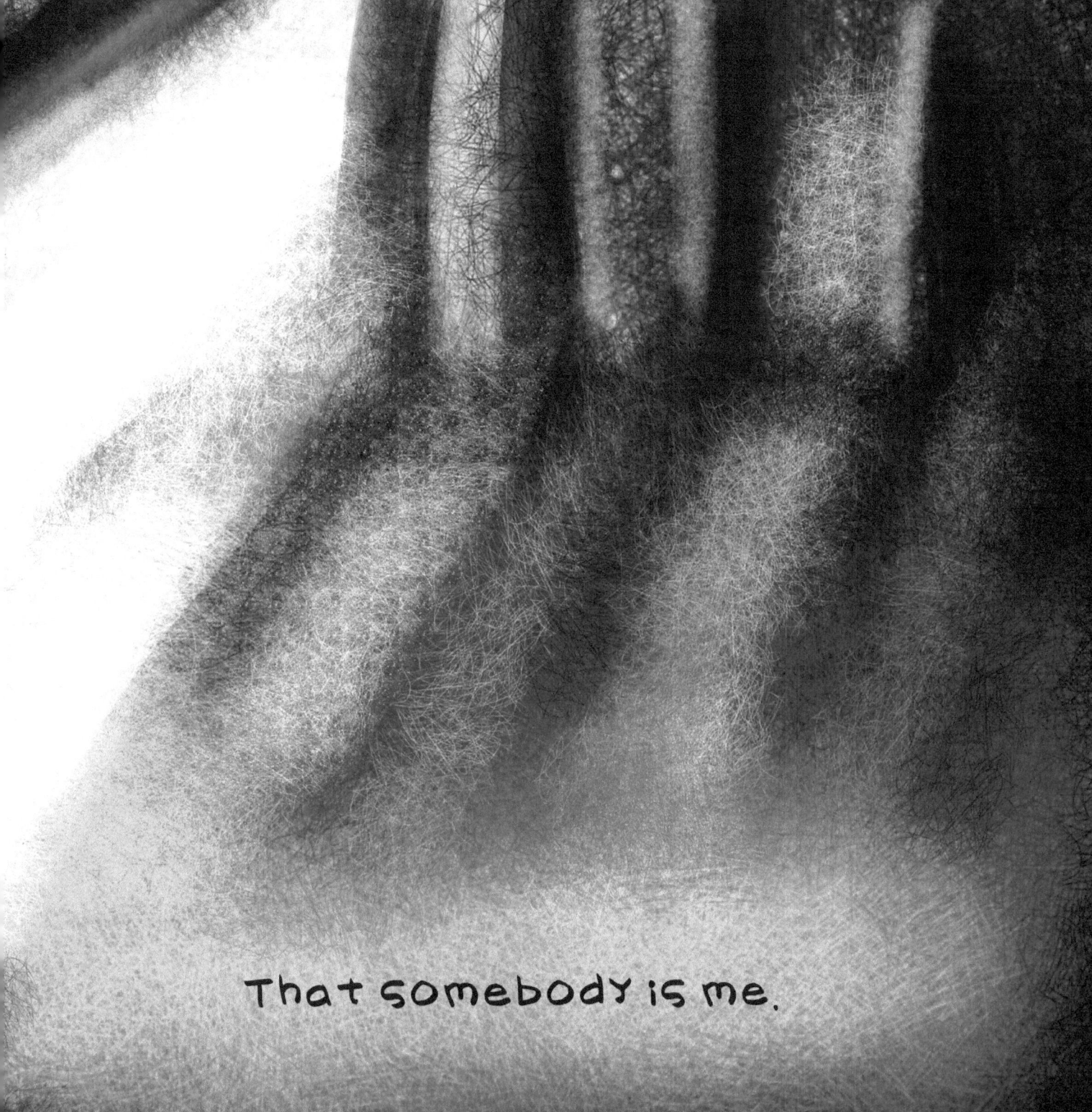

It can start right here

with only what I have.

I can choose to love.

and start to mend

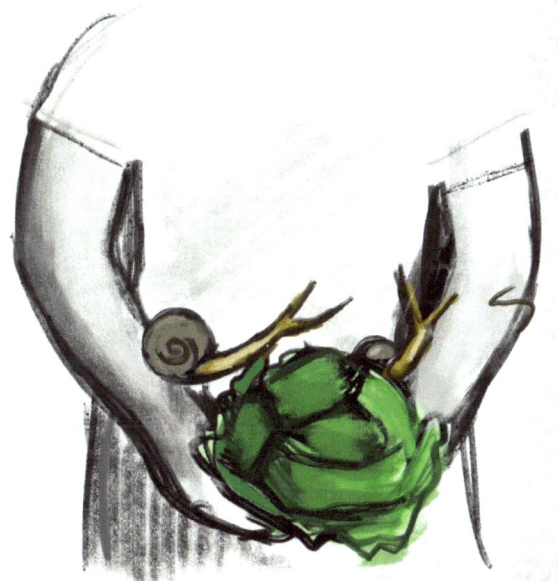

what's been broken.

where there is despair, I can spark hope.

where there is darkness, I can let light in.

where there is sadness,

I can make room for joy.

I don't have to wait until things get better.

When I comfort you,
I somehow feel better, too.

I can try to understand you

before I'm understood.

I can believe the best about you,

about us,

about what's

possible

when I open my heart and share myself.

As I let things go,

I'm set free.

Somebody needs to do something.

That somebody is me!

The Prayer of Saint Francis of Assisi

Lord, make me an instrument of Your peace:
where there is hatred, let me sow love;
where there is injury, pardon;
where there is doubt, faith;
where there is despair, hope;
where there is darkness, light;
where there is sadness, joy.

O divine Master, grant that I may not so much
seek to be consoled as to console,
to be understood as to understand,
to be loved as to love.
For it is in giving that we receive,
it is in pardoning that we are pardoned,
and it is in dying that we are born to
eternal life.

Amen.

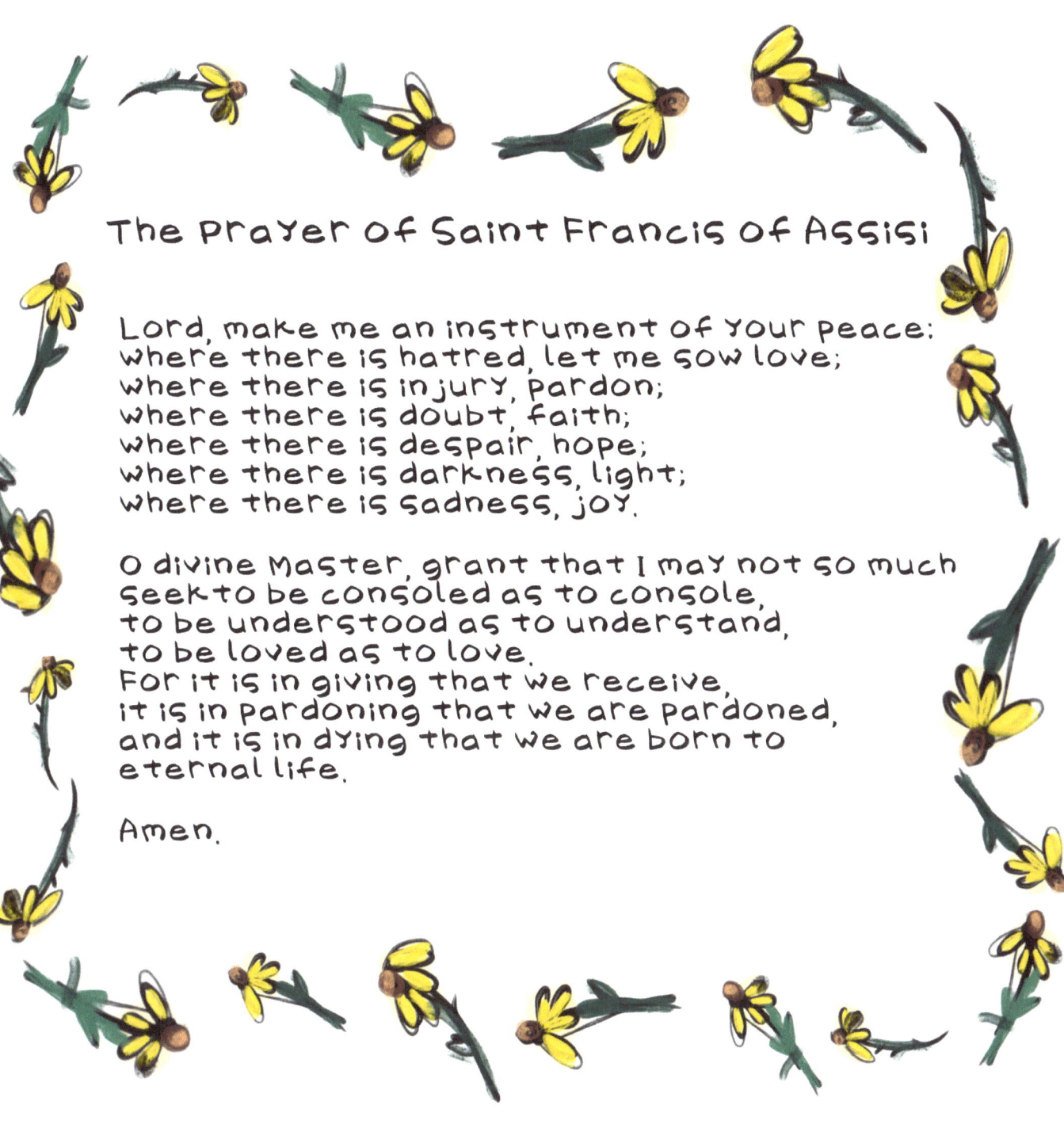

www.ingramcontent.com/pod-product-compliance
Lightning Source LLC
Chambersburg PA
CBHW041159290426
44109CB00002B/70